Owen M. Taylor

The History of Annapolis, the Capital of Maryland

The state house, its various public buildings, together with a full history

and description of the United States Naval Academy from its origin to the

present time

Owen M. Taylor

The History of Annapolis, the Capital of Maryland
The state house, its various public buildings, together with a full history and description of the United States Naval Academy from its origin to the present time

ISBN/EAN: 9783337288990

Printed in Europe, USA, Canada, Australia, Japan

Cover: Foto ©ninafisch / pixelio.de

More available books at **www.hansebooks.com**

THE

HISTORY OF ANNAPOLIS,

The Capital of Maryland:

THE STATE HOUSE, ITS VARIOUS PUBLIC BUILDINGS, INCLUDING THE SENATE
CHAMBER, WHERE GENERAL WASHINGTON RESIGNED HIS COMMISSION,
PORTRAITS, RELICS, &c. OF THE STATE, GOVERNMENT MANSION, ST.
JOHN'S COLLEGE, ST. MARY'S CATHOLIC CHURCH AND COLLEGE, ST.
ANNE'S CHURCH, PRESBYTERIAN AND METHODIST CHURCHES,
CITY AND NATIONAL CEMETERIES, FARMERS' AND FIRST
NATIONAL BANKS, CITY AND MARYLAND HOTELS,
ASSEMBLY ROOMS, COURT HOUSE, &C., &C.

Together with a full History and Description

OF THE

UNITED STATES NAVAL ACADEMY,

FROM ITS ORIGIN TO THE PRESENT TIME.

ITS BUILDINGS, GROUNDS, FOUNTAINS, CEMETERY AND PARK, CHAPEL,
MONUMENTS, LIBRARY, NEW MIDSHIPMEN'S QUARTERS,

WITH AN APPENDIX,

Containing a variety of Historical and Interesting Reminiscences, &c.

COMPILED AND EDITED BY

OWEN M. TAYLOR,

ANNAPOLIS, MD.

=

BALTIMORE:
TURNBULL BROTHERS.
1872.

INTRODUCTION.

THE Author of the following pages entertaining the belief that their publication might be acceptable to his fellow-citizens, and a generous public, has committed them to the press, in the hope that his readers may derive something of interest from their perusal. In taking this step he has had many misgivings. Diffident of his ability to invest his subject with the interest that belongs to it, he would have been loath indeed to give it publicity had it not been for the absence of any such publication.

He has gathered his material from the records within his reach. He is indebted for much of it to the "Annals of Annapolis," (which unfortunately has become obsolete,) and to the valuable assistance afforded him by Commodore Worden, Superintendent at the Naval Academy, Henry Lee Snyder, Chief Engineer at the Academy, and to Rev. William S. Southgate, of St. Anne's Church.

The undersigned bespeaks for this publication the clemency of all.

OWEN M. TAYLOR.

A BRIEF DESCRIPTION OF THE ANCIENT

CITY OF ANNAPOLIS,

AND ITS

MOST PROMINENT PUBLIC AND PRIVATE BUILDINGS, &c.

---•---

CHAPTER I.

ITS EARLY HISTORY.

Town of St. Mary's — The Capital of the Province — An Assembly called — Act of Virginia against dissenting Ministers — The Puritans leave Virginia — Take refuge in Maryland — And settle at Providence, now Annapolis — Oath of Fidelity — Mr. Thomas Greene appointed Governor in the absence of Governor William Stone — He proclaims the Prince of Wales — The inhabitants of Providence prefer the dominion of the Commonwealth — Governor Stone returns — Calls an Assembly — The Puritans refuse to attend — Governor Stone visits Providence — Returns Burgesses to the Assembly — They attend — Providence organised into a county called Anne Arundel — Murders committed by the Indians — Susquehanock Indians — Preparations against the Indians.

The town of Saint Mary's became the capital of the Province, and the first Legislative Assembly of the Province was called and held there, about the commencement of the year 1635.

Having stated this preliminary fact, and not intending to connect the history of the Province with these "annals" further than what may appear to be necessary, we will now turn to some of the causes which eventuated in the settlement of the present capital of Maryland.

In the year 1642 the Assembly of the Province of Virginia passed an Act to prevent dissenting ministers from preaching and propagating their doctrines in that colony. Under this Act the Governor and Council of Virginia issued an order that all such persons as would not conform to the discipline of the Church of England should depart the country by a certain day. Notwithstanding the laws against the Puritans in Virginia, they continued to keep up a conventicle of their members for some years, which had in the year 1648 increased to one hundred and eighteen members. At this period the government of that colony caused a more vigorous execution of the laws to be enforced against them. Their conventicle in Virginia was therefore broken up, and the members of it being driven out of that colony, were dispersed in different directions. The pastor (a Mr. Harrison) went from thence to Boston, in New England, in the latter end of this year, and the elder (a Mr. Durand) took refuge in Maryland. It is stated by one of their own members to have taken place in the year 1649, but at what time of the year we are nowhere informed. Most probably they did not leave Virginia in a body, but gradually, in small numbers, in the course of the spring and summer of this year. It is stated by Mr. Leonard Strong, in his *Babylon's Fall*, &c., that they were not invited into Maryland by Governor Stone, but by a friend of the Governor's; that they were only "received and protected." These people seated themselves at a place by them called "Providence," but afterwards "Proctors," or "The Town Land at Severn;" later still, "The Town at Proctors;" then "The Town Land at Severn where the town was formerly;" after that, "Anne Arundel Town," which was subsequently changed into "The Port of Annapolis," and finally, under its charter in 1708, was established as the "City of Annapolis."

It is alleged by the advocate of the Puritans who thus settled at Providence (Leonard Strong, before cited) that "an oath to the Lord Baltimore was urged upon this people soon after their arrival, which if they did not take they must have no land nor abiding in the Province." The oath here alluded to was the oath of fidelity, as prescribed by his lordship, and annexed to his "condition of Plantations," of 1648. They were made acquainted by Captain Stone before they came here with that oath of fidelity, which was to be taken by those who would hold any land here from his lordship; "nor had they any objection to the oath, till they were as much refreshed with their entertainment there as the snake in the fable was with the countryman's breast; for which some of them were equally thankful. But it was deemed by some of these people too much below them to take an oath to the Lord Proprietary of that Province, though many Protestants of much better quality had taken it." Although these people had thus with the permission of the Lord Proprietary's government, seated themselves within the Province of Maryland, yet it does not appear that they had immediately thereon subjected themselves to the Proprietary government of St. Mary's.

The peninsula or neck of land whereon Annapolis stands was probably uninhabited by any Europeans before their arrival; and thus secluded from the rest of the inhabitants of the Province, it is probable that, according to the usage of the Congregational Church of New England, a branch of which Church they were, a sort of hierarchical government was established by them, similar to that which had been practised by the first colonies of Plymouth, Massachusetts, and Connecticut. Neither does it appear that any grants of land or territory were made to these people, either collectively or individually, either prior to or subsequent to their arrival in Maryland, until the latter end of July 1650, when their settlement was organised as a county, under a commander and commissioners of the peace, as the Isle of Kent had been before.

In this year (1649), when Charles I. was beheaded, Mr. Thomas Greene, who was now Governor of Maryland, in the absence of Governor Stone, caused the Prince of Wales to be proclaimed in the Province, as "the undoubted rightful heir to all his father's dominions," on the fifteenth day of November. Another proclamation was also issued, of the same date, "to further the common rejoicing of the inhabitants upon that occasion," declaring a general pardon to all the inhabitants of the Province for every offence before committed.

It appears, however, that the Puritans who had just settled on the Severn did not join in the "common rejoicing;" but preferring the rule and dominion of the Commonwealth of England, just established in the mother country, to that of the declared succession of their late sovereign, Charles I., desired to be exempt from the common privilege of causing the shores of their beautiful Severn to re-echo with their "rejoicings" on this occasion.

In January 1650, Governor Stone having returned to the Province and resumed the functions of his office, convened the Legislature by proclamation, to meet at St. Mary's on the second day of April ensuing. On the day appointed the Assembly accordingly convened; but as no returns were made, nor any appearance of the freemen or burgesses from Providence, "the Governor adjourned the House till Friday next, the fifth day of the same present month."

In the meantime it appears that Governor Stone visited the new colony at Providence, probably with a view of reconciling in an amicable way the refractory Puritans to the Proprietary government; for it seems that they consented to send two burgesses to the Assembly, and the Governor himself made the return thereof as follows :

"By the Lieutenant, &c., of Maryland: The freemen of that part of Maryland now called Providence, being by my appointment duly summoned to this present Assembly, did unanimously make choice of Mr. Puddington and Mr. James Cox for their burgesses, I being there in person at that time."

Accordingly, on the sixth of April the Assembly met, and after choosing James Cox Speaker, and Mr. William Britton their Clerk, proceeded to business. We may remark here that this choice of the Speaker seems to indicate the growing strength and influence of the infant colony that had settled at Providence.

The Puritans who had founded Providence formed at this early period of their settlement a considerable population, and having sent and been represented by their burgesses or delegates at this last Assembly, and so far submitting to the Proprietary government, an Act was passed at this session, entitled "An Act for the creating of Providence into a county, by the name of *Anne Arundel County.*" The tenor of this Act was, "that part of the Province of Maryland, on the west side of the Chesapeake Bay, over against the *Isle of Kent,* formerly called by the name of Providence, by the inhabitants there residing, &c., shall from henceforth be erected into a shire or county, by the name of Anne Arundel County, and by that name be ever hereafter called." It was probably so called from the maiden name of Lady Baltimore, then lately deceased — Lady Anne Arundel, the daughter of Lord Arundel of Wardour, whom Cecilius Lord Baltimore had married.

No boundaries were assigned by this Act to the county. As the population of that part of the Province was detached from the other inhabited parts, and like *Kent Island,* was insulated from the rest of the Province, such population constituted its limits in fact, until in process of time other counties being erected adjacent thereto, defined its boundaries.

This detached colony had its inconveniences and difficulties to contend with, incident to all newly-settled places. It became thereby not only more obnoxious to the Indians, but more liable to alarm, and more easily assailed by these aborigines. Some Acts of Assembly, made at the last session of Assembly, indicated considerable uneasiness existing at this period among the colonists on account of some recent murders and captures committed among them by the natives. It appears that two of the inhabitants of Kent and Anne Arundel Counties had been lately murdered in a most cruel and barbarous manner by certain Indians. It is most probable that the Indians who committed the above-mentioned murders were the *Susquehanocks,* a powerful and warlike tribe who inhabited all that part of Maryland which lies between the Patuxent and *Susquehanough* rivers, on the western shore, and all that portion of country from the Choptank to the *Susquehanough,* on the eastern shore. This Assembly, in addition to this cautionary measure of preventing a repetition of such murders by the Indians, thought it necessary that some more effectual remedy to check such conduct of the natives should be applied, and accordingly enacted " An order providing for a march upon

2

the Indians," as follows :   " Whereas, certain Indians, this last
year, have most wickedly and barbarously murdered an English
inhabitant of the County of Kent, and another inhabitant likewise since, in Anne Arundel County, *Be it therefore ordered*,
That the Governor, with the advice of the Council, or the
major part of them, shall have power, in case such Indians
who have committed such barbarous and wicked murders shall
not be sent in after demand made of them to the Government
here, to receive such punishment as is due for such offence, to
press men and to appoint such allowance for their pay, and to
make war upon these nations of Indians refusing to deliver up
those offenders as aforesaid, as in his and their best discretion
shall be thought fit; the charge of which war to be laid by an
equal assessment on the persons and estates of all the inhabitants of this Province."

It would appear, however, notwithstanding all this preparation for an Indian war, that a considerable *trade* was still
carried on, either with these hostile Indians, or more probably
with some other tribe or tribes, who remained in a state of
peace with our colonists.

CHAPTER II.

PUBLIC BUILDINGS.

CITY OF ANNAPOLIS — Its Population — Shipping — Its Site — Its Advantages — NAVAL ACADEMY — Its Proximity to the Seat of the National Government — The State House, in which General George Washington resigned his Commission — The Treasury Department — The Government House — Portraits and Relics of the State — St. John's College — St. Mary's Catholic College and Church — St. Anne's Church — Presbyterian and Methodist Churches — City and National Cemeteries — Farmers' and First National Banks — City and Maryland Hotels — Assembly Rooms — Court House, etc., etc.

The City of Annapolis, the capital of Maryland, received its name on the 16th day of August 1708, in honor of Queen Anne, the then reigning monarch of England. The charter was granted by the Hon. John Seymour, then the Royal Governor of the Province. It is situated on the south branch of the Severn river, thirty miles south from Baltimore, and forty miles east-northeast from Washington, in latitude 38° 58' north; longitude, Washington city, 0° 31' east. Its population is about seven thousand; shipping some 8000 tons. It stands on a peninsula formed by Acton's Creek on the south, and Covey's Creek on the north; the heads of these two creeks being within a half-mile of each other. Its greatest length is little more than a mile, and in breadth something more than half a mile. It covers an area of about a hundred and sixty-three acres.

The site of the city is one of great beauty, commanding an extensive view of the Chesapeake Bay and the surrounding country, which exhibits a great diversity of landscape and picturesque scenery. The appellation of the " Beautiful City " has often been applied to her, especially when clothed in Nature's brightest livery.

Annapolis is the natal place of some of the most distinguished men America can boast of; and has the honor of being the native place of five of the most beautiful and accomplished peeresses of our mother country — the Misses Caton, grand-daughters of Charles Carroll of Carrollton.

This city is admirably adapted as a location for both commercial and manufacturing enterprises, to a greater extent than it has been favored with. Her central position between the North and the South; her proximity to the seat of our National Government; her fine and commodious harbor, which gives her great commercial advantages — all combine to recommend her to the General and State Governments for consideration. There is water bold and extensive enough for all desirable purposes; and also seven miles from the mouth of the Severn is the Round Bay, a beautiful sheet of water, which of itself presents a commodious and secure harbor for ships of war.

The public buildings are the State House, the Treasury, the Government House, St. John's College, Episcopal Church, Presbyterian Church, Catholic College and Church, two Methodist Episcopal Churches, the Farmers' National Bank, and the First National Bank, Court House, the Maryland and City Hotels, Assembly Rooms, &c., &c.

THE STATE HOUSE.

The State House is situated on a beautiful elevation in the centre of the city. It has elicited alike the admiration of the citizen, the sojourner, and the stranger, for the beauty of its structure. The main building is of brick, and the superstructure which surmounts it is of wood. The height from the base to the top of the spire is two hundred feet. From the platform of the dome, which is one hundred and thirty feet high, the spectator has one of the most delightful panoramic views to be found within the United States. It commands a view of Nature in all the beauty of poetic scenery; the ancient city, the adjacent country, the noble Chesapeake, and the Eastern Shore beyond it, for an extent of thirty miles around, break upon the view of the delighted eye.

The hill on which stands this noble edifice is enclosed by a neat and substantial granite wall, surmounted by a handsome iron railing, which is entered by three gates, one situated at the head of Frances street and in front of the building, the second to the southwest, and the third to the northeast of the circle. The main entrance to the building is through a portico of but modest pretensions, and opens into a spacious and beautiful hall, in which is had a view of the interior of the dome, the stucco-work of which was made from plaster brought from St. Mary's County.

On the right hand of the hall is the Senate Chamber. This room is judiciously and tastefully fitted up for the use of the Senators of our State. It is thirty-four feet by forty; it has a lobby and gallery for the accommodation of visitors. Persons of distinction are often invited within the bar of the Senate, where seats are provided for them. Portraits at full length of the distinguished Charles Carroll of Carrollton, Samuel Chase, William Paca, and Thomas Stone, ornament the walls. These gentlemen were the four signers of the Declaration of Independence on the part of Maryland, and were at that period all citizens of Annapolis; each of them in his day filled various posts of honor and responsibility, and shared largely the confidence and esteem of his fellow-citizens. The first-named gentleman was the last survivor of that illustrious band of patriots who signed the Declaration of American Independence. There is also in this room a portrait of the "Hero of the Cowpens," the virtuous and excellent John Eager Howard, who has with the rest of his compatriots gone to the land of his fathers, there to reap the rewards of an honorable and well-spent life. In 1788, '89 and '90, Mr. Howard was Governor of Maryland. The first and last named portraits were painted by Mr. Sully, the others by Mr. Bordley, both native artists.

There is likewise in the Committee Room adjoining the Senate Chamber a portrait of the elder Pitt, the friend of America. In this picture Lord Chatham is represented at full length, in the attitude and costume of a Roman orator, with decorations of emblematical figures expressive of his noble principles. It was painted by Charles Wilson Peale (who was

a native of Annapolis) while in England, and presented by
him in the year 1794 to his native State.

This room is still more memorable as being the spot upon
which was consummated the greatest act in the life of the
greatest man of any age. It was here that Washington, after
having rescued his country from foreign dominion and usurpa-
tion, nobly laid down his authority on the altar of liberty —
resigning his commission into the hands of Congress — (in
this connection the author will state that over the door from
the Senate Chamber to the Committee Room will be seen a
scene most instructive and interesting, that is to say, Washington's resignation of his military commission) — and in this
room, too, was ratified by the same Congress, the treaty of
peace with Great Britain, of 1783, recognising our independence.

On the left of the hall, immediately opposite to the Senate
Chamber, is the Chamber of the House of Delegates. This
apartment originally was of the same dimensions as the former,
and had also a gallery for the accommodation of spectators ;
and at that period was suspended from the walls a large
picture, presenting a full length likeness of General Washington, attended by General La Fayette and Colonel Tilghman,
his aides-de-camp, the Continental army passing in review.
In his hand he holds the articles of capitulation at Yorktown.
This picture was painted by Charles Wilson Peale, in pur-
suance of a resolution of the General Assembly of Maryland.

The Chamber of the House of Delegates has within several
years past been much enlarged and handsomely refitted, and is
capable of accommodating all its members, who sit at desks
conveniently arranged, together with the numerous spectators
who from day to day visit that body. The last three Conven-
tions to reform the organic law of Maryland assembled and
held their deliberations in this hall.

At the termination of the hall of entrance to the State
House the State Library is situated, which is appropriately
fitted up, and contains at present some twenty thousand
volumes of standard legal and miscellaneous works.

In the public hall are two stairways; the one on the right leads to a flight of stairs to the Executive Department, directly over the Senate Chamber. This room was occupied under a former Constitution of the State, and previous to the year 1838, by the Governor and Council. It has often since that period undergone repairs, and is neatly and appropriately furnished. The Executive business is now transacted by the Governor and the Secretary of State. Opposite to the door of the State Department, a stairway leads to the dome of the building.

The stairway on the left of the public hall leads to the Court-room of the Court of Appeals of Maryland, and adjoining thereto is the Clerk's office and consultation chamber of the Judges. They are over the hall of the House of Delegates. The large picture of General Washington, attended by General La Fayette and Col. Tilghman, &c., and removed from the hall of the House of Delegates, has been assigned a place in the Court-room, and is hung immediately in front of the Justices.

THE TREASURY.

Within the circle enclosing the State House on the eastern margin of the hill, stands the Treasury Department. This building is venerable as well as memorable for having been the legislative hall of the Provincial government. In the larger room, the Lower House, and in the smaller one, the Upper House of Assembly, sat for many years; such accommodations contrast strikingly with those of the present day.

COMPTROLLER'S OFFICE.

A short distance to the northeast from the Treasury Department stands the Comptroller's and Record Office. In the latter are deposited the archives of the State, together with the old records formerly in the Chancery Office, long since abolished. There is also in this building the Land Office. This, as likewise the State House, is heated by steam and lighted by gas. On the northwest of the circle is the steam apparatus. The grounds surrounding the State House are handsomely laid out and decorated with the most choice trees, shrubbery and flowers, and present an appearance in summer rarely to be seen. On the southwest of the Capitol is an ever-gushing jet-fountain of modern style, and a fish-pool of unsurpassed quality and beauty. These grounds are visited during the spring, summer, and autumn months by large numbers of excursionists from all parts of the State, who invariably leave well pleased with their visit to the ancient city.

From the State House and Episcopal Church circles, respectively, many of the streets radiate, and intersect each other at convenient points. The plan is a peculiar and an agreeable one, when viewed from some prominent point.

THE OLD GOVERNMENT HOUSE.

The *original* Government House, at least the main building thereof, was erected by Edmund Jennings, Esq., and was purchased from him by Governor Eden, when he presided over the Province of Maryland; and by whom were built the wings and long room. That edifice had a handsome court and garden, extending, with the exception of an intervening lot, to the water's edge. From the portico looking to the garden, a fine prospect regales the vision. The building consisted of two stories, and presented an extensive front; there were on the lower floor a large room on each side of the hall as you enter, and several smaller ones; the saloon on the same floor was nearly the length of the house.

On each side of the edifice were commodious kitchens, carriage-houses and stables, with spacious lots. Towards the water the building rose in the middle in a turreted shape. It stood detached from other structures, and was at the time it was permitted to stand a delightful and suitable mansion for the residence of the Chief Magistrate of our State. During the year 1869 the United States Government purchased from the State of Maryland, at a cost of $25,000, the above described

mansion, &c., and it is now incorporated within the area of the
Naval Academy, and is used as a library and lyceum, and as
offices for the Superintendent and Secretary of the Academy,
one room being used for meetings of the Academic Board.

The New Government House

Is about two hundred yards west of the State Capitol. It is
a magnificent mansion, supplied with all modern improvements,
centrally located, and was erected in 1869 at a cost of nearly
two hundred thousand dollars. Ex-Governor Oden Bowie
was the first to occupy this stately domicile.

St. John's College.

In 1784 the General Assembly of Maryland passed an Act
for founding a college on the Western Shore, and incorporated
the institution by the name of the " Visitors and Governors of
St. John's College ; " and for the purpose of providing a " permanent fund for the further encouragement and establishment
of the said College, the sum of £1750 was annually and
forever thereafter given and granted as a donation by the
public, to the use of the said College." The Legislature also
granted for the use of the institution, four acres of land (now
known by the name of the College Green), and which land had
been in the year 1744 conveyed by Stephen Boardley to
Mr. Bladen, the then Governor of Maryland. Mr. Bladen pro-
jected the present college building as a noble mansion for the
residence of the Governors of Maryland. A Mr. Duff (the
architect) came over from Scotland to superintend the construction of the building. Materials of every kind were provided equal to the spirit of public liberality, and the edifice
was nearly completed in a style of superior magnificence, when
an unhappy contention took place between the Governor and
Legislature, which increased to such a degree that at a period
when a very trifling sum would have rendered it a noble residence, the further prosecution of the design was discontinued,
and it remained for a long time a melancholy and mouldering

3

monument of the consequences resulting from political dis-
sensions. It received the cognomen of the " Governor's Folly."

The depredations of time had greatly injured the interior of
the building, which in an unfinished state continued many
years exposed to the inclemency of the weather; but the Legislature, actuated by sentiments which reflect the highest credit
on their patriotism and wisdom, having determined to endow
and found a college for the education of youth in every liberal
and useful branch of science, wisely resolved to repair the
damages sustained, and to apply the building to the purposes
of education. The agents appointed by the Legislature for
soliciting subscriptions and donations for St. John's College
were the Rev. John Carroll, the Rev. Wm. Smith, and Patrick
Allison, doctors of divinity, and Richard Sprigg, John Steret,
and George Diggs, Esquires, with power to appoint other
agents. By an Act of Assembly passed in 1785, the funds of
" King William's School," which had been founded at Annapolis ever since the year 1696, were conveyed to St. John's
College.

In thus establishing a seminary of learning at the seat of
government, our patriots and statesmen manifested their sense
of the great importance of and the happy results which would
flow from an institution of this character, under the State patronage, and how inseparably it was connected with the interest
and happiness of our people. For years the flourishing condition of St. John's fully realised the most sanguine expec-
tations of its noble and enlightened founders. Scholars and
statesmen were sent forth from her halls who have been the
pride of her own and the admiration of other States, and who
have earned for themselves the highest reputation and reflected
honor on their Alma Mater. But alas! this noble and effi-
cient monument of the wisdom of our progenitors was but too
soon to meet a sad reverse of fortune; for as early as the year
1805 we find that political discord, that horrible hydra with
its hundred heads, reared its crest against this institution, and
by an Act of the Legislature in that year the funds of the
college were withdrawn. This paralysed its energies and re-

duced it to a languishing condition, in which posture it remained until 1811, when the Legislature, partially awakened to a sense of duty and justice to the cause of education, granted $1000 annually, and again in 1821 granted to its Visitors and Governors a scheme of a lottery by which was added to its permanent funds twenty thousand dollars.

In 1831, when the efforts of its Visitors and Governors were crowned with success in obtaining the services of its then able Principal, Rev. Hector Humphreys, D. D., long since deceased, a still brighter prospect dawned upon this old and favored institution of the State. By the united and unceasing exertions of the then Faculty, Visitors and Governors of the institution, it was again placed in a prosperous condition.

The efforts thus made to revive this venerable seminary of learning could not but attract the further attention of our Legislature. In 1833 the State came nobly to the rescue of good old St. John's, and passed an Act of compromise, by which $2000 per annum, in addition to former grants, were secured to the college forever, and which the Visitors and Governors accepted in full of their legal and equitable claims; and a deed of release, enjoined by the provisions of the Act, was executed and entered upon the records of the Court of Appeals.

At a meeting of the Board of the Visitors and Governors of the College, held on the 15th February, 1834, the Principal was authorised and requested to collect subscriptions, to be applied to the erection of suitable buildings for the accommodation of students, and for the improving and extending the library and the philosophical apparatus of the institution. For the purpose of carrying this object into effect, the Principal visited several parts of the State, and succeeded in obtaining a subscription of more than twelve thousand dollars, from the proceeds of which has been erected a beautiful edifice, finished in a style of elegance that reflects great credit upon its projectors.

St. John's College stands on an eminence at the termination of Prince George Street, and is a four-storied structure, in-

cluding the basement. This building, as also the others which
form a part of the College, were used during the late war as
hospitals for the Federal army stationed at this point, since
which time they have undergone thorough repairs. A more
delightful situation was never appropriated than this for its
purposes. It is situated on the banks of the Severn, within
the limits of the city, commanding in every point of view the
most interesting and beautiful objects. The adjacent country
is open and healthy; the contiguous grounds are sufficiently
extensive for the advantages of exercise and amusement; and
the fabric contains a variety of spacious and convenient apartments for the accommodation of the professors and students.

The peculiar advantages to youth in being educated at this
seminary are numerous and evident. With respect to health, as
far as a high and dry soil with pure air will contribute to its
preservation, or restore it when impaired, few places can be put
in competition with, and none can excel it. The sessions of
the General Assembly and the meetings of the Court of
Appeals and the Circuit Court, are so obviously beneficial to
those young men who may be called to the public service, or
enter into the profession of the law, that no parent, especially
a citizen of our State, should hesitate a moment to send his son
whom he desires to become eminent in any of the professions,
to a place where he is the most likely to acquire those quali-
fications which will render him useful and distinguished as a
statesman, or afford him the greatest chance of professional improvement. Large cities often defeat the salutary purposes of
education by furnishing incitements to vice and affording op-
portunities of concealment. Annapolis is happily free from
these objections; and the discipline of this institution is such
as to prevent the student from deviating from the path of rectitude, even if so inclined. The forming of manners, so es-
sential to those who are intended for any public or private
pursuit, will keep pace with the improvement of the intellect,
and a youth when qualified to enter on the scene of action will
be enabled to perform his part with ease to himself and sat-
isfaction to the observer. If all the advantages mentioned are

united in this institution, and which it is presumed no one will dispute, why, we may inquire, should the citizens of Maryland send their sons abroad to other seminaries, instead of patronising an institution of their own? — an institution, we will venture to assert, that has sent forth to the world a constant and regular supply of alumni who, by their talents at the bar, in the sacred desk, and in our legislative halls, have proved themselves inferior to none from any other seminary in the Union.

The College Green in the Revolutionary War was used as the encampment of the French army, and also by the American troops assembled in the war of 1812. Traces of these encampments still remain, and render it an object of touching interest. Parts of it exhibit mounds raised to those who died in service; and though "no storied urn" designates the spot where the remains of any distinguished warrior repose, all being indiscriminately inhumed, yet the interest of their fate is undiminished by this circumstance when we reflect that they died in the same glorious cause.

On the grounds east of the College stands a large forest poplar or "American tulip tree," the age of which is not known. It is highly probable that it formed a part of the forest which was growing when Annapolis was first settled by the Puritans in 1649. This tree has been commemorated in verse by a distinguished graduate of St. John's (the lamented Dr. John Shaw, who was a native of our city), and is held to this day in great veneration by our citizens. Some time about the year 1839 it was accidentally set on fire. The occurrence excited as much interest in, and exertion on the part of our inhabitants to extinguish it, and save the old favorite tree from destruction, as if it had been one of the finest buildings of the city. It was truly gratifying to see the interest elicited and the delight manifested by many when the progress of the fire was arrested.

St. Anne's Church.

The present St. Anne's Church is the third building on the same site. It stands about two hundred yards west of the State House. The first church was built there about the year 1696, and was taken down to make room for the second. That was begun in 1774, and finished in the year 1792. On the 24th November of that year the building was consecrated by Bishop Claggett.

This second church building was burned in the year 1858. The fire took from some defects in the arrangement of the furnace. A fine, large bell presented to the parish by Queen Anne was destroyed with this building. Mementoes of this bell are still preserved by some of our citizens in the shape of trinkets made of the metal found among the ruins. The silver communion-vessels given to the parish were preserved, and are still in use in the church. The service consists of seven pieces, on each of which the monogram and arms of King William III. are engraved.

The present edifice was built some twelve years ago under the rectorship of Rev. J. R. Davenport, now of New York. The tower encloses in its walls a portion of that of the old church built of bricks imported from England. The interior is divided by large solid stone pillars into nave and aisles. There is a deep apsidal chancel, with six clergy stalls, organ, and abundant space for choir seats. It has a richly carved altar of gray stone, and the floor of the sanctuary is laid in pattern with enamelled tiles. There are 134 pews, of which 25 are free. The building will seat some 800 persons, and is enclosed by a neat and substantial iron railing. Within this enclosure are several sculptured tombs, which contain the remains of the Tasker family. There is also a monument erected in memory of some of the members of the Carroll family.

St. Mary's Catholic Church

Is a large and handsome structure, and is situated on the Duke of Gloucester Street, on grounds donated to the church by the venerable and generous Charles Carroll of Carrollton during his lifetime. It has not been erected many years, and its appearance both internally and externally displays great taste and judgment. The interior especially is very handsome and appropriate, and the general arrangement is convenient and comfortable. Connected with this church is St. Mary's College of the Redemptorists. This Society was established at Annapolis in 1853, under the auspices of the Rev. Gabriel Rumpler. An addition to this college was built in 1859, when the very Rev. Michael Müller was Rector of St. Mary's Church.

This institution is one of three through which candidates desiring to become missionary priests of the Society have to pass. The first is St. James College, Eager and Aisquith streets, Baltimore, where the candidates remain about six years; they are then sent to Annapolis, where, according to their intellectual abilities, they stay from two to four years; afterwards they go to St. Clement's College, Ilchester, Howard county, Maryland, where they continue their studies for five or six, more years. After their promotion to the priesthood they return to Annapolis for a six months' trial and course of instruction in pastoral duties.

THE METHODIST CHURCHES.

Methodist Episcopal Church, first charge, is situated on the north side of the State House circle. It is a large, commodious and handsome building, with basement and vestibule, and has adjoining it a brick parsonage for the minister in charge. It was erected in the year 1859.

The second charge was built in 1870, and is situated on Maryland Avenue, a short distance from the Post Office. It is a one-story building, and is designated as Wesleyan Chapel. Its interior is, like the outside, plain but becomingly neat, and is capable of accommodating some four hundred persons.

The Presbyterian Church

Is located on the southwest side of Gloucester Street, and was erected some twenty-five years since. It is a plain but neat building, and is capable of accommodating some three hundred persons. The basement of this edifice is occupied by the Female Grammar School.

The Banks.

The Farmers' National Bank is situated at the corner of West Street, fronting the Church circle. It consists of one story, and is of singular form externally, though the interior, particularly the banking room, is well calculated for the purposes for which it is intended.

The First National Bank is located on the corner of Main and Gloucester Streets, and also fronts the Church circle, and adjoining the Maryland Hotel. It may be truly said of these institutions that they have ever been and still are considered as sound and as safe as any other banking establishments in this country.

The Court House

Is quite a modern edifice, and stands on the southwest of the Church circle. As you enter there is a spacious hall, on each side of which are two commodious offices. The one on the right hand is occupied by the Register of Wills, the other by the Clerk of the County, and at the end of the hall is the Court Room. This is a fine spacious room, and well suited to the purposes to which it is appropriated. On the second floor are the Orphans' Court Room, the Sheriff's Office, Surveyor's Office, Jury Rooms, and a room used by the Commissioners of the County. The front roof of the building, compared with the rear, exhibits the appearance of wings. It is enclosed by a substantial wall surmounted by a neat iron railing, and is lighted by gas and supplied with water.

The City Hotel

Stands at the corner of Main and Conduit Streets, and has been in the occupancy of a number of individuals since its establishment as such. The old building, as it is termed, originally belonged to and was occupied by Mr. Lloyd Dulany as his residence. It is two stories high; the new building is three, and a large building of three stories has recently been added, extending back to the Duke of Gloucester Street. The present worthy and enterprising proprietor has added greatly to its appearance and comfort. This structure with its appendages covers a large space of ground. It is an excellent establishment, and in every respect well calculated for the comfortable accommodation of travellers and others who make it a place of abode or resort. The rooms are large and airy, the table constantly supplied with all the delicacies of the season, and a corps of obliging and honest waiters always in attendance.

The Maryland Hotel.

This establishment is of recent origin, its existence only dating back some three years. It is a very commodious, beautiful and comfortable structure, and built according to modern architecture and with an eye to its convenience and central location. It is situated at the head of Main Street, and near the Church circle, and within a short distance of the Depot. It is an incorporated institution, and since it has been in operation has received a share of public patronage.

The Assembly Rooms

Are on the Duke of Gloucester Street, and is a spacious edifice. It was built since the late war on the site of the "Old Ball Room," which was used a portion of that period as a Provost-Marshal's Office and Guard House, and from means awarded by the General Government to the city for its use and occupation. Its main room is large and of elegant construction, and when illuminated shows to great advantage. It

4

contains several apartments, which are rented out for balls, concerts, lectures, public meetings, &c. A room is set apart as the place of meeting for the corporate authorities of the city. In the basement is the Office of the City Police and Watch-House.

The Post Office

Is situated at the corner of State House Circle and Maryland Avenue, occupying a portion of the first story of Temperance Hall.

CHAPTER III.

THE NAVAL ACADEMY.

Front entrance,—termination of Maryland Avenue.

THE NAVAL ACADEMY — Its Foundation — The Academy Grounds — Cemetery and Park — Public Garden — Buildings, &c.— New Midshipmen's Quarters — Water Supply — Monuments — The Library — Storekeeper's Department — Mess Arrangements, &c.— Baths, Barber Shop, Laundry — Band — Hops and Balls — Boat and Ball Clubs, &c. — Evening Parades — Marine Corps — The Daguerrean Gallery — Department of Steam Enginery — Memorial Tablets.

In the year 1845, it being found desirable to establish a permanent institution for the instruction of midshipmen in the United States Navy, a board, of which Commodore Isaac Mayo, U. S. Navy, was President, was ordered by the Hon. George Bancroft, Secretary of the Navy, to select a site for a *Naval School.*

After examining various localities, Annapolis was chosen as being the most eligible place.

On the 10th of October 1845 the school was formally opened by Commander Franklin Buchanan, with the following named officers as *Instructors,* viz: Lieut. James H. Ward, U. S. N., Professors Henry H. Lockwood, William Chauvenet, and Arsene N. Girault ; *Surgeon,* John A. Lockwood ; *Chaplain,* George Jones, and Passed Midshipman Samuel Marcy. These officers constituted the first " Academic Board."

The following departments were at once organised, viz :

Department of Gunnery and Steam.............	*Lieutenant Ward.*
" " Mathematics, Navigation, &c..........	*Prof. Chauvenet.*
" " Natural and Experimental Philosophy..	*Prof. Lockwood.*
" " Chemistry........................	*Surgeon Lockwood.*
" " History and English studies..........	*Chaplain Jones.*
" " French and Spanish................	*Prof. Girault.*

Infantry tactics was also practically taught by Prof. Lockwood. Past Midshipman Marcy was assigned to the department of Mathematics as an assistant.

All candidates for admission to the grade of midshipman
were, after this date, sent to the Naval School to be examined
by the Academic Board, and if found qualified, were admitted
on probation, receiving from the Secretary of the Navy acting
appointments as midshipmen. These constituted the "*Junior
Class*," and remained at the school under instruction until the
Navy Department required their services at sea.

The "*Senior Class*" was composed of midshipmen who, having seen sufficient sea service to entitle them to it, were pre-
paring for their *final examination* for promotion.

Occasionally other midshipmen were, between their cruises,
sent to the "school" for short periods. These were assigned
to the Senior or Junior class according as they were qualified.

The regular term of the Senior Class was one academic year
of nine months; and as the course of study was to many but a
review of branches that they had studied at sea, a very considerable amount of ground was gone over by the higher sec-
tions, and a not inconsiderable amount by the lower. The
academic year commenced in October, and terminated in June,
when the final examination of the Senior Class took place.

A Board of five Captains and Commanders was each June
convened, who conducted the examination in seamanship; and
after combining the results of this examination with that in
academic branches by the Academic Board, assigned numbers,
or, in other words, the "order of merit" to the class, and con-
ferred the "*passing certificates*." The same officers also acted
as a "Board of Visitors," to witness the examination of the
Junior Class, and to examine into and report upon the discipline and general condition of the institution.

The Midshipmen of the date of 1840 were the first who
were graduated at the Naval School, finishing their course in
June 1846, and were followed in regular succession by the subsequent dates until the change to the *four years' course*. The
date of 1841 being very large, was divided into three classes,
who came in successive years, the last division being graduated
in 1849; the date of 1842 were graduated with them, but
classed separately. There were no appointments made in 1843

and 1844, and the date of 1845 followed the last division of the '41's and '42's.

In 1850 a board consisting of Commodore W. B. Shubrick, Commander F. Buchanan, Commander S. F. Dupont, Commander George P. Upshur, Surgeon W. S. W. Ruschenberger, and Professor William Chauvenet, and General Brewerton, then Superintendent of the Military Academy at West Point, as a consulting member, was convened by the Hon. Secretary of the Navy, and under a code of regulations prepared by them the Naval School was, on the first day of July of that year, erected into the

UNITED STATES NAVAL ACADEMY.

Commander (now Rear Admiral) Cornelius K. Stribling was the first Superintendent under the new régime, relieving Commander Upshur, who had held the command since March 1847.

In November of the following year (1851) the *four years' course* was adopted, under a revision of the regulations, made by the Academic Board, and approved by the Hon. Secretary of the Navy, the date of 1851 being the first to come under the new system; a portion of this date were *advanced*, and six members of it accomplished the course in three years. The modified course was still retained for previous dates, that of 1850. being graduated in 1856.

In November 1853 Captain Stribling was relieved by Commander (now Rear-Admiral) Louis M. Goldsborough, who in turn was relieved in September 1857 by Captain (now Commodore) George S. Blake, since deceased.

In May 1861, in consequence of the breaking out of the rebellion, it was found necessary to remove the Academy to Newport, R. I. The midshipmen were accordingly embarked on board the School-Ship *Constitution*, Lieutenant-Commanding George W. Rodgers, and sent to that point. The steamer *Baltic* was employed to transport the officers and others with their families; the library and such other movable property,

&c., of the Academy, as it was thought advisable and necessary to remove. The first class was graduated-without examination, a portion of them having been detached before the removal of the Academy from Annapolis, and upon its arrival at Newport the remainder of the first, and all of the second and third classes, were detached and ordered to sea duty. Fort Adams was assigned to the use of the Academy by the War Department, but was found entirely unsuited to the purpose. The midshipmen were therefore quartered on board the *Constitution* for the summer, and in September the Atlantic Hotel, a large and commodious building, was hired, fitted up for the purpose, and used as quarters until the return of the Academy to Annapolis. The two school-ships *Santee* and *Constitution* were moored alongside the wharf upon Goat Island in the harbor, and the fourth class and also the third were quartered on board of them.

In September 1865 Commodore Blake was relieved by Rear-Admiral (now Admiral) D. D. Porter as Superintendent, and during the same month the Academy was, in conformity with a joint resolution of Congress, restored to its former home at Annapolis, the grounds and buildings having been vacated by the War Department a few months previously. In a very short time after, all traces of the late occupation by the army had been obliterated.

On the first of December 1869, Commodore John L. Worden relieved Admiral Porter, and is at present Superintendent of the Academy.

ACADEMY GROUNDS.

The limits of the grounds originally transferred to the War Department were as follows: The northwestern boundary was coincident with the path now leading from the upper end of the mess-hall to the middle gate; the southwestern extended from the water past the building now used as the Paymaster's office, a line which is still distinctly marked by a row of trees; the embankment just in rear of the midshipmen's quarters, then the shore of the river, formed the northeastern boundary;

while the shore line from the southeastern, or bay point, extended from the Gymnasium (then called Fort Severn) in a sort of crescent form, passing near the mulberry tree in the lower parade-ground, and thence bowing out and terminating where the angle at present is in the sea-wall. During the year 1851 the sea-wall was built, and the space between that and the shore was filled in during that and the following years.

The first acquisition to the grounds was made by purchase about the year 1847, and included that portion of the grounds lying directly northwest of the former limits, and bounded on the northwest by the road leading from the upper gate to the river; the southwest boundary of this was a continuation of the line bounding the original grounds on the same side, and is also distinctly marked out by the same row of trees.

The second acquisition added all that portion of the grounds above the middle gate which is now enclosed in the walls of the Academy. This purchase was made about the year 1853. The sea-wall on the Severn side was built in 1853, and the space between that and the old shore was filled in with earth from a high hill which existed near where the new Midshipmen's Quarters now stand.

In 1867 a lot of 9½ acres of ground was purchased from St. John's College beyond the walls, which has not yet been enclosed; also in 1868 and '69 the farm known as "Strawberry Hill," and the land between that and the Severn River and "Graveyard Creek," making in all 114¼ acres, were purchased. Communication with this new addition was established by means of a substantial drawbridge thrown across the creek.

CEMETERY AND PARK.

On a high point of land in this last purchase has been laid out a cemetery for the burial of officers and seamen and others belonging to the navy. Beyond the cemetery there is a handsome park. The park and cemetery consist of alternate wood and lawn, with considerable diversity of level. Winding woods and paths have been laid out in very tasteful manner,

making all parts accessible.   So attractive are these two places
that although the improvements are scarcely yet begun, they
have become a favorite resort for the people in the vicinity, a
large number of persons visiting each every pleasant day.
The woods and paths already completed measure three miles,
and it is contemplated to lay out two miles more.   These are
covered with shells, which have been obtained at an ex-
tremely small cost.

Public Garden.

The remainder of Strawberry Hill is devoted to garden
purposes, for the benefit of the officers and midshipmen.   A
large quantity of fruits and vegetables have been already
gathered, although only a commencement has thus far been
made.   A very considerable diminution of the midshipmen's
mess-bill will result from the operation of the plan when fully
developed.

Since the return of the Academy to this place much has been
done in the way of ornamenting and improving that portion
of the grounds lying inside the walls ; fountains have been
erected, roads and paths tastefully laid out, low places filled
in, trees, shrubs, and flowers planted.   The ground in rear of
the Midshipmen's Quarters, which was found a barren waste,
has been reclaimed, and made one of the most ornamental
parts of the yard.

Buildings, &c.

Of the buildings originally transferred by the War Department there remain at present the Superintendent's house,
buildings Nos. 16, 17, 18, and 19 (known as Superintendent's
Row), and the building used as the Paymaster's office, nor
were any of these in their present condition when first received ; the Superintendent's house has been altered and re-
paired on three different occasions, the others were all one-
story houses, and were raised upon about the year 1848.

There were some few barracks, offices, &c., standing when

the School was first established, one of which, situated across the Parade, between the Superintendent's house and the spot where the Recitation Hall now stands, was used as a Recitation Hall and Chapel. The others were on the ground where the Midshipmen's Quarters now stand, and were occupied by the midshipmen.

The construction of the southern half of the present Mess Hall was commenced soon after the opening of the school and was completed in 1847, the second story being used as a Lyceum and Library. In 1853 the Mess Hall was enlarged to its present dimensions. The whole cost as nearly as can be ascertained was $17,809.94.

The Midshipmen's Quarters were next commenced. Block No. 1 was completed in 1850, at a cost of $7,200.00; No. 5, early in 1851, cost $10,312.07; No. 2, late in 1851, at a cost of $7,663.45; and Nos. 3 and 4, in 1853, the former costing $7,981.20 and the latter $10,007.62. The Recitation Hall was completed in 1853, at a cost of $19,656.46. The building now used as a Store, but originally built as a Laboratory and Armory, was erected about 1853, at a cost of $7,020.31. The structure upon the walls of old Fort Severn, now used as a Gymnasium, but originally as a battery for great gun exercises, was finished in 1851, and cost $6,433.30. Gas and steam for heating were introduced in 1853, the works for the same being built at an original cost of $28,044.28, and certain additions afterwards made at a cost of $8,500.00. The Observatory was completed about 1854, at a cost of $4,695.75. The Gunnery Building, originally a chapel, was completed the same year, costing $3,292.86. A brick building in the lower part of the yard, recently occupied as a store, engine-house, and residence for the band-leader, was also built in 1851, at a cost of $4,264.44. Building No. 20 (a wooden structure) was originally a hospital and store, in the middle of the lower parade-ground; it was rebuilt at a cost of $1,000.00 on the building of the new Hospital about 1857. The new Hospital cost $13,000.00.

The row of buildings known as Officers' Row was com-

5

menced about 1855, those nearest the hospital being first built. The last were not completed until 1860. The cost of the different blocks was as follows: Block No. 1 (house of Commandant of midshipmen) $5,000; houses 2 and 3, one block, $10,000; houses 4 and 5, one block, $10,000; houses 6 and 7, one block, $9,000; houses 8 and 9, one block, $10,069.18; houses 10 and 11, one block, $10,069.18; houses 12 and 13, one block, $11,000; houses 14 and 15, one block, $11,000. The two buildings occupied by the bandsmen were built in 1860, at a cost of $1500 each.

A row of officers' quarters also stood until about 1859, facing on the street which then existed, and the site of which is still marked by the row of trees running about southeast and northwest through the centre of the upper part of the yard; the lower end of this row was just above where the Japanese bell now is, and the upper end rested on the road now leading from the upper gate to the river; there were also two houses facing on that road, then a street of the City of Annapolis; part of these buildings were purchased with the ground upon which they stood, and part were built. The Herndon Monument is on the site of one of the buildings of this row. These buildings were torn down from time to time, and the materials from them used in constructing the new Officers' Row and the bandsmen's quarters.

Since the return of the Academy to this place in 1865, the following buildings have been constructed, viz: One block (two houses) of officers' quarters, Nos. 21 and 22, at a cost of $10,000. A building for the department of Steam Enginery was completed in 1866 at a cost of $21,000. The new Chapel was completed in 1848, at a cost of $40,000. During the present year there has been finished, at a cost of $11,000, a new building for the department of Natural and Experimental Philosophy. A Daguerrean Gallery was completed in 1868 at a cost of $2500.

The Academy has also during the year obtained by purchase, at a cost of $25,000, possession of the building lately occupied as the mansion of the Governor of Maryland. It is now used as a Library and Lyceum, and as offices for the Superintendent and Secretary of the Academy, one room being used for meetings of the Academic Board.

NEW MIDSHIPMEN'S QUARTERS.

A new building, designed to accommodate two hundred midshipmen, was erected about a year since. It is a four-story structure with basement and attic, and is composed of a centre building fifty-seven feet six inches square, and two wings each one hundred and sixteen feet nine inches long, by forty-five feet three inches deep; the whole is surmounted by a dome and clock-tower, the latter supplied with a clock having four dials, to be illuminated at night. The base of the dome is surmounted by a promenade gallery, from which a most magnificent view is to be had of the surrounding country and of the Chesapeake Bay.

In the basement, under the east wing, there is a kitchen fifty-eight feet long by forty-two wide, with large store-room, servants' hall, &c., attached; under the main building, a pantry, boiler-room (for supplying steam with which the building is heated,) a coal-cellar and a bath-room; under the west wing are bath-rooms. A corridor of twelve feet in width runs the entire length of the main building at right angles to the corridor; there are stairways at the extremities of each wing, and in the main building these continue to the highest story.

On the first floor in the west wing there is a mess-hall one hundred and two feet long, and occupying the entire depth of the wing, with a store-room attached; in the main building there are four rooms each eighteen by twenty-one feet, one of which is a pantry, one an office for the Commandant of midshipmen, one an office for the officer in charge, and the fourth a reception-room for visitors. In the west wing there are seven recitation rooms, each twenty-eight by fourteen feet, and eight water-closets. There is the same arrangement of hall, corridors and stairways on this floor as in the basement.

On the second floor the west wing is divided off into twelve dormitories, one servants' room, and one baggage room, each fourteen by fourteen feet; the main building into four recitation rooms twenty-one by eighteen feet each; and the east wing into dormitories of the same dimensions as those in the west wing. The corridors on this and the upper floors run the entire length of the building; the halls and stairways are the same as the first floor. The wings of the upper stories are the same as the second; the main building in each is divided into five rooms, to be used as recitation rooms, &c. There are entrances in front, rear, and at each end of the building, each covered by a portico. There is a graceful iron veranda extending across the entire front of the building.

WATER.

Water was introduced into the Academy on the completion of the Annapolis water-works in 1867. Each house in the yard, and all the public buildings, are supplied with hydrants. There are also several in the yard to be used in case of fire.

MONUMENTS.

The following monuments stand on the grounds of the Academy. The first was erected in 1848, the purpose of which will be seen by the inscriptions quoted below. It is entirely of marble, and consists of a pedestal six feet four inches square and two feet high; upon this rests the base, two feet nine and a-half inches square and four feet high, upon two opposite sides of which are the inscriptions. This monument stood originally in the centre of the parade ground, and was moved to its present position.

To Passed Midshipmen
H. A. CLEMSON
and
J. R. HYNSON,
Lost with the U. S. S. Brig Somers,
Off Vera Cruz,

December 8th, 1846,

This Monument is erected

by

Passed and other Midshipmen

Of the U. S. Navy,

As a tribute of respect.

1848.

———

To Midshipmen,

J. W. PILLSBURY

and

T. B. SHUBRICK,

The former wounded off Vera Cruz,

July 24th, 1846,

The latter killed at the Naval Battery

Near Vera Cruz,

March 25th, 1847,

While in the discharge of their duties,

This Monument is erected

by

Passed and other Midshipmen,

As a tribute of respect.

1848.

The other two faces are ornamented by bronze foul-anchors; upon the base rests a capital five feet four inches square, supported at each corner by a gun resting on the base; the whole is surmounted by a pyramidal shaft seven feet high, the four faces of which are ornamented by laurel wreaths in bronze, and under them respectively the names —

CLEMSON, HYNSON, PILLSBURY, SHUBRICK.

The Herndon Monument was erected in June 1860 by subscription, by officers of the Navy, to the memory of Commander William L. Herndon, U. S. Navy, who lost his life September 12th 1857, while commanding the mail steamship Central

America, in a gallant attempt to save the lives of his passengers, his ship having been wrecked. The monument consists of a base and shaft; the former six feet square and three feet high; the latter, which is pyramidal in form, eighteen feet high, four feet square at the base, and one foot six inches square at the top. On the face of the shaft is inscribed —

HERNDON.

and on the opposite side —

September 12th, 1857.

The Naval Monument was "erected to the memory of Captain Richard Somers, and Lieutenants James Caldwell, James Decatur, Henry Wadsworth, Joseph Israel, and John S. Dorsey, who fell in the several attacks made on the City of Tripoli, in the year of our Lord 1804, and in the 28th year of the Independence of the United States." It was erected in 1808, and stood originally in the Washington Navy Yard. During the occupation of Washington by the British in the war of 1812-'14, this monument was considerably defaced by them, and bore for many years afterwards, by authority of Congress, an inscription commemorative of the fact. Some years after its erection this monument was removed to the Capitol grounds in Washington. In July 1860 it was removed by authority of Congress to this place, and erected on the grounds of the Naval Academy, where it now stands.

LIBRARY.

The formation of a Library was commenced soon after the opening of the Naval School in 1845, by the transfer of a small number of books from the Navy Department. These were at first deposited in the Superintendent's office; soon after a hall room was fitted up in the old building, then used as a recitation hall, &c., which room was used until the completion of the Mess Hall, when the second story of that building was assigned as a Library and Lyceum.

Congress early commenced to make small annual appropriations for the increase of the Library. The exact date of the first I have not been able to ascertain.

On the enlargement of the Mess Hall to its present dimensions, the second story was divided into three rooms, two of which were used for the Library, and the third for the Lyceum; a large number of curiosities, models, &c., having by that time accumulated. Numerous flags, trophies of naval victories in various wars, were deposited in the Lyceum.

On the removal of the Academy to Newport, the books, &c., were boxed up, and thus remained until after the return of the Academy to this place, when the library was located in its old quarters; but during the year 1869 the first floor of the (late) Governor's Mansion has been handsomely fitted up as a library, and the books, &c., transferred to it.

Very large accessions have been made to the library during the last four years, more especially of works on professional subjects; all the branches taught at the Academy, and their kindred subjects, being very largely represented. The best professional and other periodicals published in this country and in Great Britain are taken.

The officers and midshipmen have free access to the Library, the Librarian or assistant being constantly in attendance during authorised hours to issue and receive books. The whole number of volumes is at present about fifteen thousand.

A valuable collection of coins, of ancient and modern curiosities from all quarters of the globe, shells, &c., was recently bequeathed to the Academy by the late Captain Percival Drayton, U. S. N.

A valuable collection of American minerals has been received, donated by Hon. Joseph Wilson, Commissioner of the General Land Office of the United States.

A valuable acquisition to the library, recently made by purchase, consists of copies in plaster of celebrated pieces of statuary and busts of statesmen, generals, naval officers, poets, painters, and others. There is also in the Library, transferred from the Navy Department, a number of paintings representing naval engagements, together with portraits of the following naval officers, viz: Admirals Enoch Hopkins, Stewart, and Farragut; Commodores John Paul Jones, Preble, David Porter, Biddle, McDonough, Decatur, O. H. Perry, Jacob Jones, Rodgers, and M. C. Perry.

A handsome *ornithological* collection is being made, which already numbers one hundred and fourteen specimens, and many more are in course of preparation.

Storekeeper's Department.

All articles required by the students, such as books, stationery, clothing, bedding, toilet articles, &c., are furnished by the Storekeeper on requisition, approved by the Superintendent.

Until within the past two years civilians held the position of Storekeeper, and were allowed a certain percentage upon all articles furnished to midshipmen. At the present time the Storekeeper is required by law to be detailed from the list of paymasters of the navy, and has authority, with the approval of the Secretary of the Navy, to procure clothing and other necessaries for the midshipmen in the same manner as supplies are procured for the navy. These are issued at cost prices, with a small percentage to cover losses.

The old "Laboratory" has been recently converted into a Government Store, the building formerly occupied as such being found altogether too small and incommodious for the purpose.

Mess Arrangements, &c.

A Commissary is attached to the School, whose province it is to subsist the midshipmen. A board of officers, appointed by the Superintendent, audit the accounts of the Commissary, decide upon the "bill of fare," and determine the amount of compensation which shall be received monthly by the Commissary from each midshipman; this averages at present $22 per month.

The Mess Hall is a commodious, well-ventilated, and well-lighted building, with suitable kitchens, bakeries, store-rooms, &c., attached.

The midshipmen are divided into mess-crews, each commanded by a first and second captain. Each crew has its special table, and each midshipman a particular seat, those of the captains being respectively at the head and foot of the tables. A regular formation takes place before each meal and at the end; the crews one by one are marched into the Mess Hall, each person taking his place behind his chair; when all are in, grace is said by the Cadet Lieutenant-Commander, after which the word " seats " is given. The officer in charge presides at every meal, and no student is permitted to leave the room without his permission; when it is observed that all have finished, the word " rise " is given, the crews are marched out and dismissed.

BATHS.

There are hot, cold, and vapor baths in the Academy for the use of the midshipmen, each one of whom is required to take a bath at least once a week. Regular bathing hours are assigned to each gun's crew, which is marched to the bathhouse under the orders of its captain. Each midshipman takes the room assigned to him, and is allowed to remain sufficiently long to complete his bath, when the gun-captain gives the word "dress"; as soon as all have complied with that order, the crew is marched out and dismissed. An attendant, for a small consideration from each midshipman, furnishes towels, soap, &c., and keeps the house in order.

BARBER SHOP.

There is a Barber's Shop in the Academy and one on board the *Constitution.* Each midshipman who requires to be shaved pays the barber —— a month; and others paying —— a month for hair-cutting, shampooing, &c.

LAUNDRY.

Each midshipman is required every Monday morning to gather his soiled clothes into his clothes-bag, and make out a list of articles in duplicate, one to retain and one for the laundry ; the clothes are then taken by the servants to the laundry, and when done up, are returned. Three dollars a month is at present paid by each midshipman for his washing.

BAND.

There is an excellent band, composed of twenty-eight musicians, attached to the Academy, which is required to play every morning and evening for an hour, and also for drills, dress-parades, &c. Many of the musicians also play on reed and stringed instruments, forming a very fine orchestral band for hops and balls.

HOPS AND BALLS.

During the academic year hops are given once a month by the officers and also by the midshipmen ; these occur on Saturday evenings, and terminate by half-past eleven.

About the eighth of January of each year a grand ball is given by the graduating class, and on the twenty-second of February a dress hop by the second class. The balls and hops are given in the Gymnasium, which is very well adapted for the purpose. Great skill and taste have hitherto been displayed by the midshipmen in decorating the Gymnasium for the balls ; using flags, arms, evergreens, &c. Two of the rooms in the Store Building are used as dressing-rooms, and others when necessary. These hops are believed to have a very refining influence upon the young gentlemen, are certainly very attractive to officers, and to the guests present.

BOAT AND BALL CLUBS, &c.

Great attention is paid to physical training, for the furtherance of which purpose encouragement is given to athletic sports and exercises in the Gymnasium.

There is a Base Ball Club in each class ; the members practise as much as their duties will allow them to do, and many have attained very great skill. Match games occur frequently between the different classes, and occasionally with clubs from other cities, resulting generally in victory to the Academic Club.

There has been a Boat Club in the first and one in the second class each year, using hull boats ; thus far the classes have pulled against each other only, resulting in first-class time. The Academy is well supplied with boats of the ordinary navy patterns, of which the midshipmen have free use. On application by a sufficient number to the Commandant of midshipmen, he appoints one of the members coxswain, the others being subject to his orders for the time being. He is held responsible for the return of the boat in good condition, and for the observance of regulations.

Evening Parades.

A very attractive feature in the routine of the Academy is the dress parade, which occurs every evening during the session except Sundays, and except during the most inclement part of the winter. The battalion comprises all the midshipmen, under their cadet officers, organised into eight companies, the whole commanded by the assistant in the Department of Gunnery, &c., who is specially charged with infantry drills. The band, reinforced by the musicians belonging to the marine guard, is under the charge of a drum-major, and parades with the battalion.

Numerous visitors from the City of Annapolis witness these parades, finding in them an unfailing source of attraction. The midshipmen are quite as well instructed in infantry tactics as in the other branches of their profession, as was shown at a competition drill with the corps of cadets at West Point, where they were acknowledged to have excelled the latter in the manual of arms, though it was claimed the cadets were the most accomplished in marching.

Marine Corps.

Within the past two years the Marine Station at the Naval Academy has been made a permanent post, which is now in successful operation. Every morning at 9 o'clock there is a dress parade and guard-mounting by the marines, and on Mondays they have a review and inspection at 10.30 A. M. There is also a daily drill in the forenoon on week days.

The Daguerrean Gallery

At the Naval Academy is in successful operation, and has been since its establishment in 1868, under the auspices of Vice-Admiral (now Admiral) Porter, then Superintendent of the Academy. It is a commodious brick building, and is located on the northeast margin of the Academy grounds, and in the rear of the Engineer's department and laboratory.

The Department of Steam Enginery.

At the foot of the main avenue leading into the Academy grounds, near the sea wall, is a large building known as the department of Steam Enginery. It stands back from the ordinary foot pavement, leaving room for an enclosure, which is handsomely ornamented with a fountain surmounted by a statue of Neptune. The entrance gate is composed of guns captured from the British frigate " Confiance" during the last war with England, and the grounds otherwise ornamented with flower vases and the trophies of war. The front of the building bears a beautiful monogram in blue and gold. Entering by the middle door, the stranger has presented before him a scene that is at once glittering and bewildering. He instinctively hesitates to step upon the spotless, highly polished floor. Massive wrought-iron columns, whose surfaces reflect a thousand images, support the broad ceiling. All the surroundings are glittering and bright in this apartment, called the Model Room. Upon a large pedestal in the centre of the room are erected two beautiful models of marine engines, one a

working beam with paddle wheels attached, and the other what
is known as an oscillating engine. These are complete, and
can be put in operation by means of compressed air contained
in a tank beneath the floor. At the extreme end of the room
stands a perfect working model of the latest type of marine
engine as applied to men-of-war, which is very curious and interesting, being provided with plate-glass coverings to the principal parts, through which its interior machinery may be seen
in full operation. To the right and left, on all sides, the eye is
dazzled by a maze of attractive objects, including delicate instruments and a variety of curious specimens, altogether bewildering to the stranger who is unacquainted with their uses
The surrounding walls too are enriched with peculiar paintings
done in white upon a dull black ground, which makes them
conspicuous from opposite sides of the broad room.

This apartment is also used for general lectures to an entire
class when occasion calls for them. On either side are offices, one
for the use of the Chief Engineer, and the other for assistant
instructors. Passing through a doorway beyond the offices,
we enter the main body of the building, a room about one
hundred feet long and forty wide. A large open gallery supported upon polished wrought-iron columns, and surrounded
by a handsome brass rail, admits light from above, whilst
from the centre of the ceiling overhead depends a chandelier.
A neat iron floor extends throughout this vast room. Our
bewilderment amidst the surroundings of the first room is now
absorbed in astonishment at the principal object here presented
before us. Upon a raised platform is erected the ponderous
machinery of a ship-of-war, complete in all its details, from
the boilers in which the steam is generated to the powerful
propeller which imparts motion to the ship. This is no
model, but the actual thing itself as originally constructed for
practical use. Nothing can exceed the neatness of this beautiful piece of workmanship. Two boilers at the farther end
of the room are used in generating steam for putting the engines in motion, whilst the other pair are made accessible,
having the inner surfaces painted white and illuminated with

gas, for purposes of instruction. On either side of this room are extensions containing machine and blacksmith shops, store-rooms, &c., also a room containing a handsome steam fire-engine for use in case of fire within the Academy walls. Ascending by the wide stairway to the second floor, we get an excellent view at a glance over all the glittering objects below. Upon this floor are four comfortable recitation-rooms, where the students recite daily when not receiving practical instruction in the engine-room; also a room for drawing, and a model shop, where models are made as required to illustrate what is not made clear in the text.

In this department Cadet midshipmen are taught not only the theoretical part of marine steam enginery but the actual manipulation in practice.

MEMORIAL TABLETS.

Inserted in the walls of the Chapel are handsome tablets bearing the following inscriptions:

Lieut. Commander ALEXANDER SLIDELL MACKENZIE, killed in battle with savages, Formosa, June 13, 1867, aged 26 years. Erected by the officers and men of the United States Asiatic Squadron.

This tablet was gotten up in Italy, and manufactured out of the best Italian white marble.

———

To the memory of Professor WILLIAM H. WILCOX, U. S. N., Head of the Department of Mathematics of the United States Naval Academy. Died August 20, 1870, aged 47 years.

A faithful and talented officer, whose death is regretted by all who knew him.

This tablet is erected by the officers and professors of the U. S. Naval Academy, Oct. 1870.

———

In memory of Lieut. JOHN G. TALBOT, U. S. Navy, PETER FRANCIS, Quartermaster, JOHN ANDREWS, Coxswain, JAMES MUIR, Captain of the Hold, all of the U. S. S. *Saginaw*, who were drowned Dec. 19, 1870, while attempting to land on the Island of Kauai, in the North Pacific Ocean, after a boat voyage of fifteen hundred miles, voluntarily undertaken in search of aid for their wrecked shipmates on Ocean Island.

To commemorate their adventurous voyage, in admiration of their hero-ism, and to keep alive the remembrance of their noble and generous devotion, this tablet is erected by their shipmates and by officers of the U. S. Navy.

"Greater love hath no man than this, that a man lay down his life for his friends."

.

Hon. Jeremiah Townley Chase.

The Hon. Jeremiah Townley Chase was born in Baltimore Town, May 1748. He was from an early period of his life until nearly the close of it, a public man, in various important departments, in all of which he acquitted himself with honorable and distinguished reputation.

He took an early and decided part in the arduous, awful and long doubtful contest with Great Britain, in support of the violated rights of his country, which terminated in the independence of America and her emancipation from a foreign yoke. During the whole period of that awful conflict he exhibited the most active patriotic zeal, undeviating rectitude, and unshaken firmness. At the commencement of his public services he was appointed a member of the first committee of observation in Baltimore town, where he then resided, and was a private in one of the first military companies raised in Maryland. In February 1775 he was elected by Baltimore county, of which the town was then a part, a member of the Convention of this State, and in 1770 a member of the convention which formed the constitution and government of this State, and was one of that body which united in the Declaration of Independence on the part of Maryland.

After the formation of the Government he was elected, and continued to be a representative of Baltimore town until his removal to Annapolis in 1779, and was elected a member of the Executive Council, in which capacity he continued to serve to the end of the Revolutionary War; the active and important services of which Executive in procuring supplies of flour and cattle for the American army received the acknowledgments of General Washington. He was a member of Congress in 1783, when the father and saviour of his country closed his glorious career by the resignation of his commission. And in 1784 he was appointed one of the Executive Committee of that body to act in the recess of Congress. During all the awful scenes and alarming vicissitudes of the Revolutionary War he never deserted his post, nor shrunk from the faithful and vigilant discharge of his duty.

After the close of the war, and the treaty of peace with Britain which ratified and established the high destiny of America, he was elected a member of the Convention of Maryland, which passed on the adoption of the Constitution and system of national government which was finally ratified.

In 1789 he was appointed a judge of the General Court of this State. On the abolition of that court he was appointed chief judge of the third judicial district, and chief judge of the Court of Appeals. In June 1824 he resigned his office of judge, for reasons assigned in his communication to the executive. The dignity, firmness, ability, and impartiality of his conduct in his judicial capacity are too much matters of recent notoriety and general recollection to make any further detail necessary.

7

APPENDIX.

In the year 1769 the General Assembly appropriated the sum of £7500 sterling to be applied to the building of the present State House on the site of the old State House, which was destroyed by fire in the year 1704. The foundation-stone was laid on the 28th day of March, 1772, by Governor Eden. On his striking the stone with a mallet, which was customary on such occasions, tradition informs us there was a severe clap of thunder, although a cloud was not to be seen, the day being clear and beautifully serene. In 1773 this building was covered with a copper-roof, and in 1775 this roof was blown off during the equinoctial gale, and the water is said to have risen three feet perpendicular above the common tide during the storm. The dome was not added to the main building until after the Revolution. The architect of this building was a Mr. Joseph Clarke. Mr. Thomas Dance, who executed the stucco and fresco work on the interior of the dome, fell from the scaffold just as he had finished the centre piece and was killed.

An historian, in speaking of the American theatre, admits that Annapolis has the honor "of having erected the first theatre, the first temple to the dramatic muse." Of this fact there can be no doubt, for as early as the year 1752 a theatre was built here, and in which was performed some of Shakspeare's best plays. In the *Maryland Gazette* of June 18th, 1752, appears the following advertisement:

By permission of his Honor, Benjamin Fasker, Esquire [the then President or Governor of the Province], *at the new Theatre, in Annapolis*, by the company of commedians *from Virginia*, on Monday next, being the 22d of this instant [June], will be performed "The Beggars' Opera ";

likewise a farce called the "Lying Valet," to begin precisely at seven o'clock. Tickets to be had at the printing-office. Box 10s., pit 7s. 6d. No persons to be admitted behind the scenes.

It appears that this theatre was suspended for several years; for on Saturday evening, the 18th of February, in the year 1769, we find that this theatre was again opened by the American company of comedians with the tragedy of "Romeo and Juliet." This company appear to have been held in high estimation by the citizens of Annapolis for their performances, especially of the tragedy of "Richard III."

Governor Eden succeeded Governor Sharpe immediately on his arrival, and continued to govern the affairs of the Province until 1776, when he returned to England, in consequence of the Revolution and the formation of the Provisional Government of Maryland, which was at this period established. Governor Eden is represented to have been a gentleman "easy of access, courteous to all, and fascinating by his accomplishments." When he had taken his departure his property was confiscated. In 1784 he returned to Annapolis to seek the restitution of his property. He died soon after his arrival, in the residence of the late Dennis Claude, now occupied by Mayor Fendall. He was buried under the pulpit of the Episcopal Church on the north side of Severn, within two or three miles of Annapolis. This church was many years ago burned down.

A correspondent writing a letter dated Annapolis, February 20, 1770, to a friend in England, says: "On Saturday last our little city appeared in all its splendor. It was the anniversary of the Proprietary's birth. The Governor gave a grand entertainment on the occasion to a numerous party; the company brought with them every disposition to render each other happy, and the festivity concluded with cards and dancing, which engaged the attention of their respective votaries until an early hour. I am persuaded there is not a town in England of the same size of Annapolis which can boast a greater number of fashionable and handsome women; and were I not satisfied to the contrary, I should suppose that the majority of our belles possessed every advantage of a long and familiar intercourse with the manners and habits of your great metropolis."

Annapolis has always been celebrated for the elegance and beauty of her female population, and the compliment paid to them in 1770 is equally true at the present time.

The building occupied by General Luthur Gittings, and opposite the residence of Hon. George Wells, on Charles Street, is said to be the most ancient house now standing in the city. It was used as a printing-office of the *Maryland Gazette* at its establishment. The house in which the cashier of the Farmers' National Bank resides was formerly a tavern, and kept by a Mr. William Reynolds. The small brick house on Doctor's Street, now in the occupancy of Judge Hunter, was a stocking manufactory; it was regarded as a great curiosity, but did not succeed.

West Street, then called Cowpen Lane, had at this period, 1752, but three houses built on it. The most considerable one was a tavern; it was afterwards used as a circulating library. It was formerly the residence of Chancellor Johnson, and is now owned by Mr. Joseph Bellis, and is known as the National Hotel. The house in which the Misses Cowan live, and that formerly known as "Hunter's Tavern," were both erected about this time. The next house built on that street was the Hallam Theatre. It stood where Adams Express Company hold their office. The building now owned and occupied by Judge Mason was built by Governor Ogle as a family residence; additions and improvements were made to it by his son.

In 1764 the "Old Ball-room" (on the site of which the New Assembly Rooms are erected) was built from the proceeds of a lottery drawn here for that especial purpose.

The winter of 1765 was one of uncommon severity. On the 5th of February a very merry set of gentlemen had a commodious tent erected on the ice, between the town and Greensbury's Point, where they had an elegant dinner, &c., and in the afternoon diverted themselves with dancing of reels on skates and divers other amusements.

St. John's College was opened and dedicated on the 11th of November, 1789, with much solemnity, in the presence of a numerous and respectable concourse of people.

The magnificent mansion now owned and occupied by Miss Hester A. Chase, on Maryland or the Naval Academy Avenue, is among the most ancient and prominent structures of our city. It was erected about the middle of the 17th century by the venerable Samuel Chase, one of the illustrious signers of the Declaration of Independence. The building immediately opposite, and now occupied by Judge Robinson, of the Court of Appeals, was built some years subsequently by a Mr. William Hammond.

The dwelling-house now occupied by Judge Chas. S. Welch, on Hanover Street, was built in the year 1763 by an English gentleman named Thomas A. Rutland. The Episcopal rectory on the same street, and also the house belonging to and occupied by Mrs. Tilton, on Maryland Avenue, with others now standing, were built in the same year by the same individual.

The residence of the late Dennis Claude, situated on an eminence in the southern part of the city, and now occupied by Major Fendall, was built by Dr. Scott of the British army in 1760; these figures are still to be seen cut on the fireplace. It was built after the style of English manor-houses, and is enclosed by a large brick wall, embracing three acres of ground.

The former residence of the late Hon. James Murray, on the outskirts of the city, and now in the occupancy of James R. Howison, Esq., was built in the year 1762 by Mr. William Hammond, an Englishman.

All these relics of antiquity were built of brick imported from England.

On the northeast margin of the State House Hill is mounted a great curiosity in the shape of an "old cannon" taken out of St. Mary's River in the year 1633, and presented to the

State by the Rev. Joseph Carbury.   This was one of the
cannon brought to Maryland by the first settlers under Lord
Baltimore.   This relic, as may be supposed, is very unlike in
every particular those of the present day, and is a centre of
attraction to strangers who visit the " ancient " city.

www.ingramcontent.com/pod-product-compliance
Lightning Source LLC
Chambersburg PA
CBHW021642270326
41931CB00008B/1128